8-2001

Happy Birthday
Grams!
We love you very much!
♡

Anne Mahler

The wonder of
grandparents

C.R.Gibson®
FINE GIFTS SINCE 1870

All images © Hulton Getty Picture Collection.
Picture research by Jon Wright.
Design by Keith Jackson.
All text, unless otherwise attributed, by David and Rebecca Pickering.

Developed by Publishing Services Corporation, Nashville, Tennessee.

Published by C. R. Gibson®
C. R. Gibson® is a registered trademark of Thomas Nelson, Inc.
Nashville, Tennessee 37214
Printed and bound by L. Rex Printing Company Limited, China

ISBN 0-7667-6756-6
UPC 0-82272-46686-9
GB4153

The wonder of
grandparents

"A
grandparent's
arms are always
open
wide..."

"...They make you **brave** enough to step out on your own."

"Grandparents have time to make life sparkle."

"Meet the **true** romantics – you're never **too** old to fall in **love**."

"Start learning now, kid – it takes a lifetime to get this good!"

"For some of us,
the older we get,
the younger we
are."

"When **I** was younger I had **inhibitions** – now I know **better.**"

"My age is like the winter – frosty but kindly."

– William Shakespeare

"Who knows the best stories?"

"Who **knows** the **best** games?"

"Grandparents,
that's
who!"

"The **body** may need an extra **forty winks,** but..."

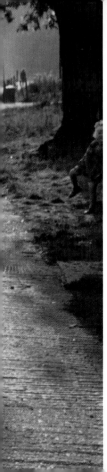

"The **heart** that **loves** is always **young.**"

– Greek proverb

"The love of a grandparent will stay with a child forever."

"You help us with
our future, by teaching
us your past."